T0060410

BOWIE

A MICHAEL ALLRED COLORING BOOK

Based on the unauthorized graphic biography
BOWIE: Stardust, Rayguns & Moonage Daydreams

Co-written by Michael Allred and Steve Horton, and originally colored by Laura Allred

INSIGHT EDITIONS

San Rafael • Los Angeles • London

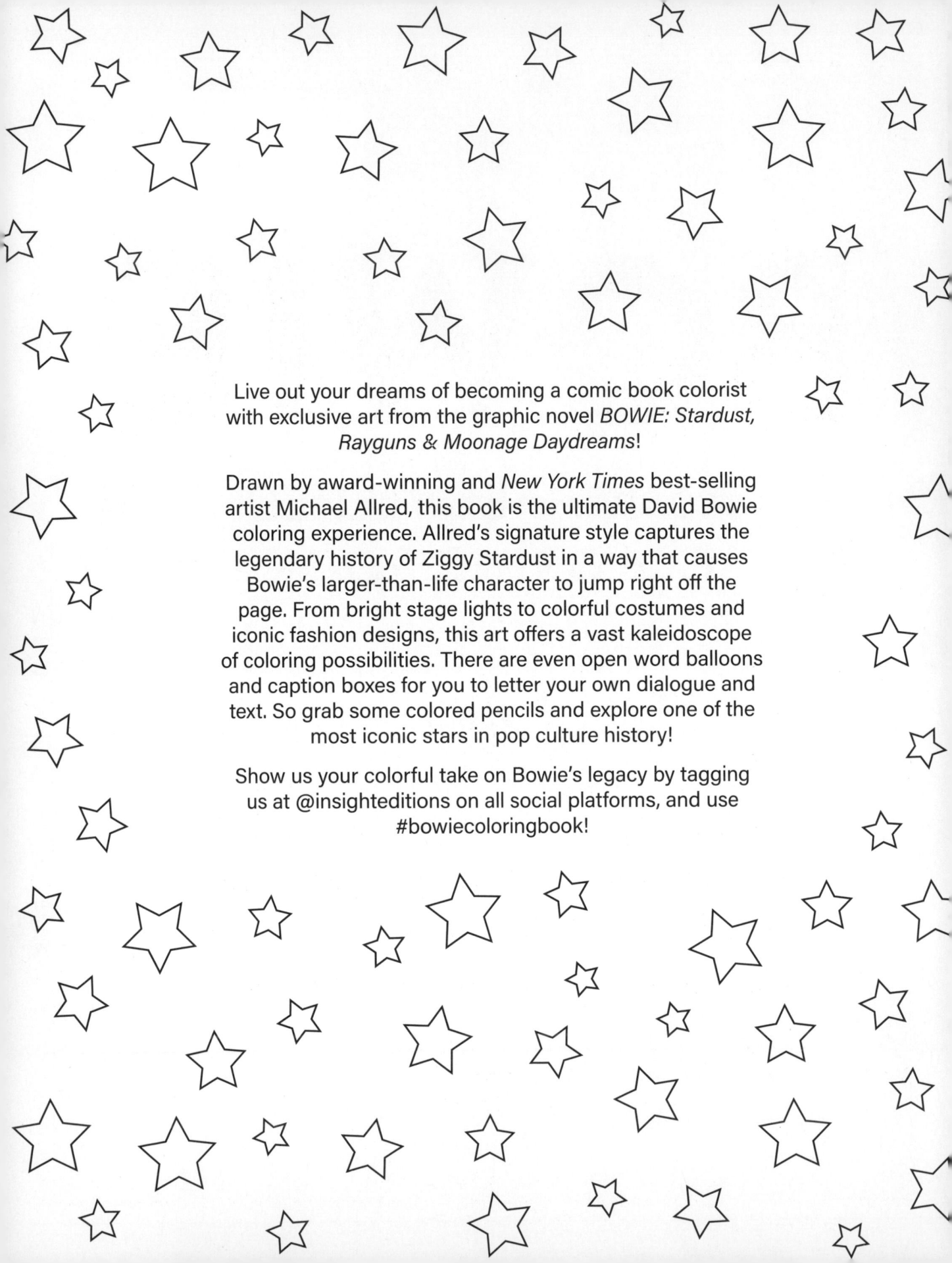

Live out your dreams of becoming a comic book colorist with exclusive art from the graphic novel *BOWIE: Stardust, Rayguns & Moonage Daydreams*!

Drawn by award-winning and *New York Times* best-selling artist Michael Allred, this book is the ultimate David Bowie coloring experience. Allred's signature style captures the legendary history of Ziggy Stardust in a way that causes Bowie's larger-than-life character to jump right off the page. From bright stage lights to colorful costumes and iconic fashion designs, this art offers a vast kaleidoscope of coloring possibilities. There are even open word balloons and caption boxes for you to letter your own dialogue and text. So grab some colored pencils and explore one of the most iconic stars in pop culture history!

Show us your colorful take on Bowie's legacy by tagging us at @insighteditions on all social platforms, and use #bowiecoloringbook!

BOWIE!
THE SPIDERS

ALL
RED

TELEPHONE

BOWIE!
STARDUST,
RAYGUNS,
& MOONAGE
DAYDREAMS
ALL RED

ODEON
FROM 8 PM WE'RE ALL
WORKING TOGETHER
WITH DAVID BOWIE
SMITH
ODEON
HAMMER
NO RE-ADMISSION
NO RE-ADMISSION
NO RE-ADMISSION
NO RE-ADMISSION

PEEL SLOWLY AN
Andy Warhol

Sooner or later
they're going to get it.
They called them
The Virgin Soldiers
COLUMBIA PICTURES & CARL FOREMAN present
but not for long.

David Bowie
David Bowie
DECCA
WHAT KIND OF A FOOL AM I
ANTHONY NEWLEY
Stereo
SOLID STATE

MAJOR TOM
GC GC GC
MAJOR TOM

MAJOR
TOM

DAVID BOWIE

David Bowie
The man who sold the world

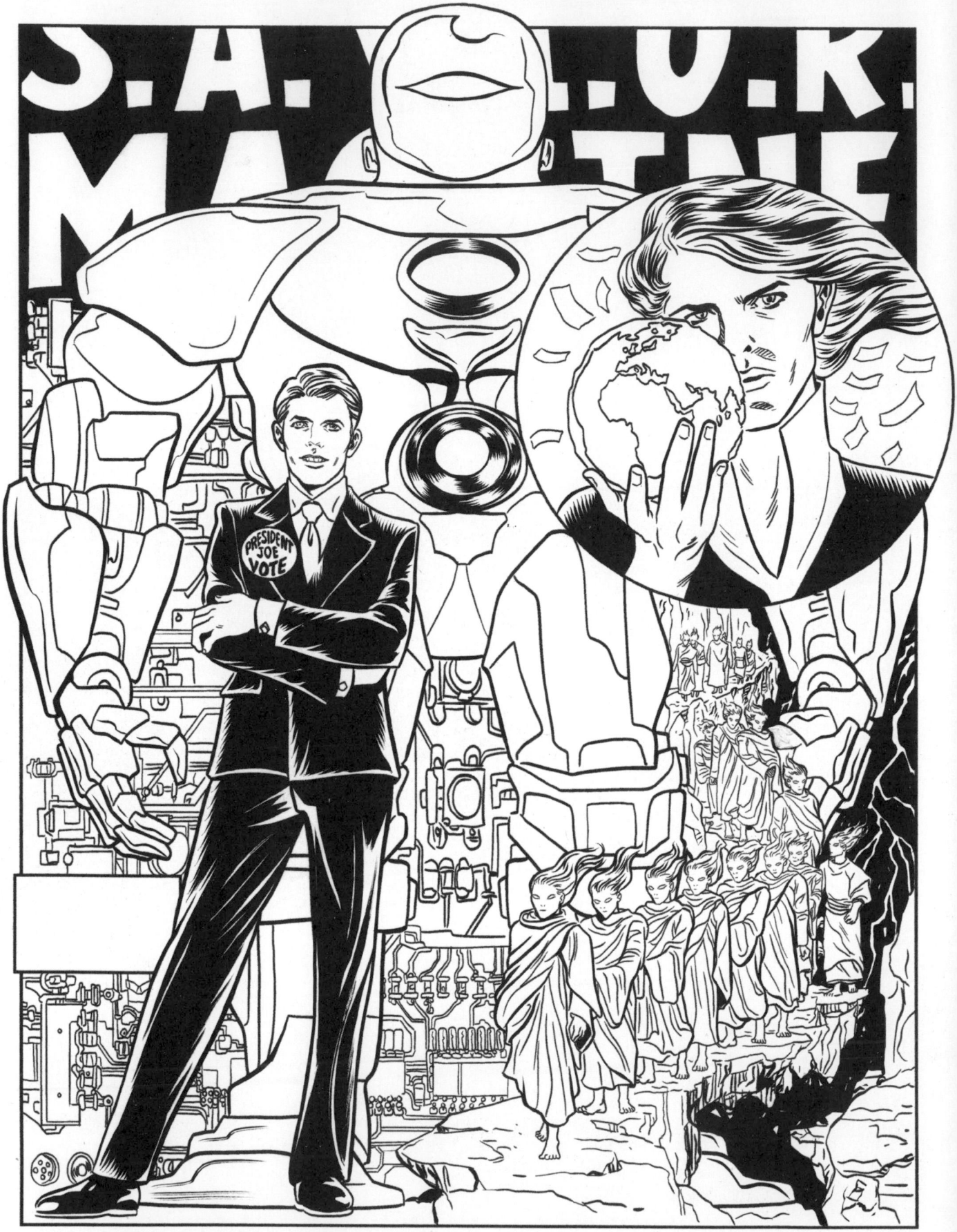
S.A.L.U.K.
MACHINE
PRESIDENT
JOE
VOTE

MARKS & SPA

I WANNAH BE YER DAWG!

LAST SHOW
LAST SHOW

DAVID BOWIE
HUNKY DORY
RECORDED ALCOHOLICALLY and hatched in my dark bathroom with
the help of Mr. Ronson, Mr. Woodmansey, Mr. Wakeman, Mr. Bolder
and Mr. Ken Scott who fed them pills, pints and pints of beer.
SIDE ONE
*1. Changes
2. Oh! You Pretty Things followed by Eight Line Poem
3. Life on Mars?
*4. Kooks
*5. Quicksand
*6. Fill Your Heart
(Biff) Andy Warhol
2. Song for Bob Dylan
3. Queen Bitch
4. The Bewley Brothers
5.
SIDE TWO
(INSPIRED BY FRANKIE)
(for small z.)
(SOME KIND WHITE LIGHT ROCK GROUP) WITH THANKS
This album was Produced by KEN SCOTT
(assisted by the action)
Remixed by KEN SCOTT
at Trident Studios London
Richard Wakeman is an exclusive recording artist of A&M Records Inc.
The musicians on my album are:-
Michael Ronson who played guitar and did the arrangements marked thus *
Woody Woodmansey playing an excellent round of drums
Trumpets Trevor Bolder bass same
Richard Wakeman on piano
I played some guitar the saxophones
and the less complicated piano parts.
(Inability).
Mick and I agree that the Fill Your Heart arrangement owes one hell of a lot to Arthur G. Wright and his proto-type
Front cover photo Brian Ward
Back cover photo GEORGE by UNDERWOOD
Front cover art work by TERRY & HIS PARTNER
my good friends at MAIN ARTORY (London)

HAPPY 25TH, DAVID

Melody Maker
ARY 22 1972
7p weekly
USA 30 cents
RIMSON
BEAK UP
ll tour
Bowie
Oh You Pretty Thing
hohner headline '72

THE TOBY JUG

HANG ON TO YOURSELF!

...HE THINKS EE'D BLOW AH MINDS...

EARTH WAS REALLY DYING

DAVID BOWIE
STARMAN
b/w Suffragette City
A GEM PRODUCTION
RCA
VICTOR
Singer who is shot on

WGM

THEHZ A STAAAAAHMAN-
WAITEEENG IN THA SKYEE-

history wallchart
WILL DAVID BOWIE COMMIT ROCKANROLL SUICIDE TO BECOME A SUPERSTAR?
BOB DYLAN: BRINGING SOME OF IT ALL BACK HOME
OU REED: HE CHUCK RRY OF THE VENTIES?
STAR·MAN
HI.
Rainbow
MICK JAGGER
ZOOM!
ELTON JOHN
ROD STEWART
ALICE COOPER
#4
4

ROLLING STONE
Issue No. 121
November 9, 1972
Are You Man Enough for David Bowie?
The Doug Sahm/Bob Dylan Sessions
The Primal Elvis Presley
Narcs at Sea: The Pleasure Cruise That Turned into a Night of Terror

BOWIE
Space
Oddity
RCA
International
THE MAN WHO
SOLD THE WORLD
DAVID
BOWIE
QUARTZ

THE
SPIDERS

SPACE ODDITY
SLATE 1
TAKE 1

ZENITH

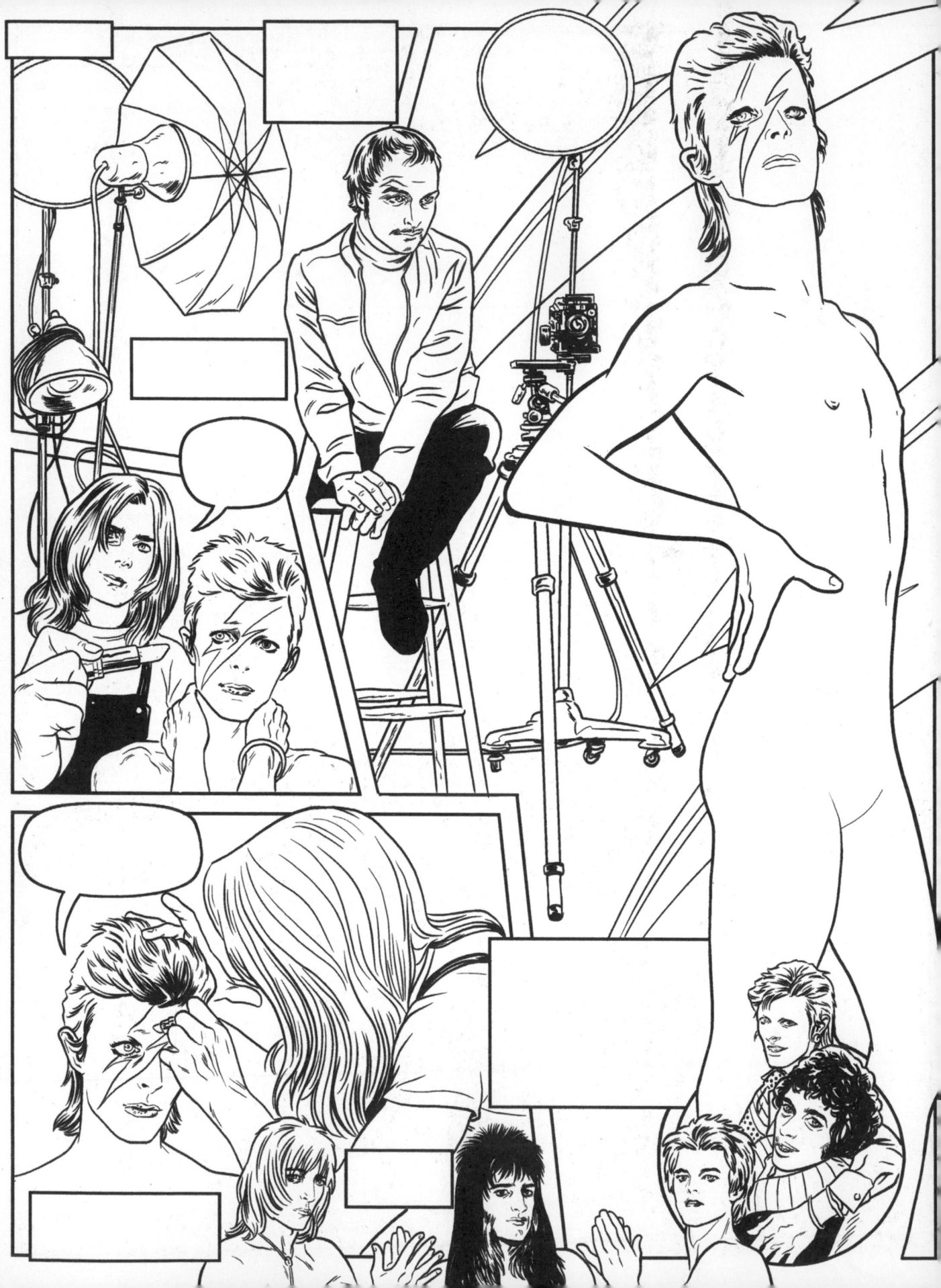

BETTE MIDLER
STEVIE WONDER
MICK JAGGER
SALVADOR DALI
JOHNNY WINTER
TRUMAN CAPOTE
TODD RUNDGREN

ようこそ
BOWIE
DAVID BOWI
ALADDIN SANE

ЫЙ
ВАГ

EXIT

LIFE ON MAR?
SLATE 1
TAKE 2

BOWIE
ODEON
HAMMERSMITH
ROCK & ROLL IS HERE TO STAY
CLUB 81, INC. PRESENTS
BOB DYLAN
DONT LOOK BACK
EXCLUSIVE PREVUE - 2 WEEKS ONLY
AUGUST 11-27

SPIDE

THE BEATLES

THE
SPIDERS

BOWIE PINUPS
MAINMAN
MICK RONSON

BOWIE

JOHN LENNON • MOTT The HOOPLE • DRA
America's Only Rock 'n' Roll Magazine
CREEM

BOWIE
KENT
BOWIE/DIAMOND DOGS
Sidesone
1. Future Legend (1:20)
2. Diamond Dogs (3:06)
3. Sweet Thing (5:23)
4. Candidate (3:03)
5. Sweet Thing (2:38) (movie)
6. Rebel Rebel (4:31)
Side two
1. Rock'n Roll
2. Width of the
3. 1984 (3:16)
4. Big Brother
5. Chant of the Circling Steel Family (1:49)
Tony Newman
Aynsley Dunbar
Herbie Flowers
Willie Garson
Bowie ... Guitar, Saxes, Moog
Written, arranged and produced by Bowie
*(Except Rock 'n Roll with me; Words by
Music by Bowie/Peace)
Engineer-Keith Harwood
Tracks 1-5. Side one, 3,4,5. Side two,
mixed by Bowie and Visconti
Tracks 6. Side one, 1,2. Side two,
mixed by Bowie and Keith Harwood.
Strings on 1984 arranged by Tony Visconti
Guitar on 1984 - Alan Parker
Recorded at Olympic and Island Studios,
and
Studio L Ludolf,
Machineweg 8-12,
Hilversum, Holland
Design: AGI
Cover-Painting: Guy Peellaert
Inside Photograph: Lee Black Childers
RCA
The
STRANGEST
LIVING
BOWIE
DIAMOND DOGS

MILITARY ARCHIVE COMMAND

POLICE DEPARTMENT
ROCHESTER, N.Y.
59640
LUST FOR LIFE!
LUST FOR LIFE!
THE ELEPHANT MAN

4
8
5
5
1
The Next Day

INSIGHT
EDITIONS
PO Box 3088
San Rafael, CA 94912
www.insighteditions.com

Find us on Facebook: www.facebook.com/InsightEditions
Follow us on Twitter: @insighteditions

© 2020 by Michael Allred. All rights reserved.

Images from the Graphic Novel *BOWIE: Stardust, Rayguns & Moonage Daydreams* by Michael Allred, Steve Horton, and Laura Allred.

Published by Insight Editions, San Rafael, California, in 2020.

No part of this book may be reproduced in any form without written permission from the publisher.

Library of Congress Cataloging-in-Publication Data available.

ISBN: 978-1-64722-217-8

Publisher: Raoul Goff
Associate Publisher: Vanessa Lopez
Creative Director: Chrissy Kwasnik
VP of Manufacturing: Alix Nicholaeff
Designer: Amy DeGrote
Associate Editor: Holly Fisher
Senior Production Editor: Elaine Ou
Production Associate: Eden Orlesky

ROOTS of PEACE REPLANTED PAPER

Insight Editions, in association with Roots of Peace, will plant two trees for each tree used in the manufacturing of this book. Roots of Peace is an internationally renowned humanitarian organization dedicated to eradicating land mines worldwide and converting war-torn lands into productive farms and wildlife habitats. Roots of Peace will plant two million fruit and nut trees in Afghanistan and provide farmers there with the skills and support necessary for sustainable land use.

Manufactured in China by Insight Editions

10 9 8 7 6 5 4 3 2 1